For Arthur, Lucas, and one to come

**Text and Images Copyright © by Little Stitches Books**

**No part of this book may be reproduced in any manner whatsoever without written permission except in the case of brief quotations embodied in critical articles and reviews.**

**Large Font text is suitable for younger children.**
**Smaller Font text is suitable for more advanced readers.**

**Be the first to hear about new releases and join the Mailing list at LittleStitchesBooks.com**

--------------------------------------------------
**ISBN: 978-1-0692837-2-6**
--------------------------------------------------
**First Edition**

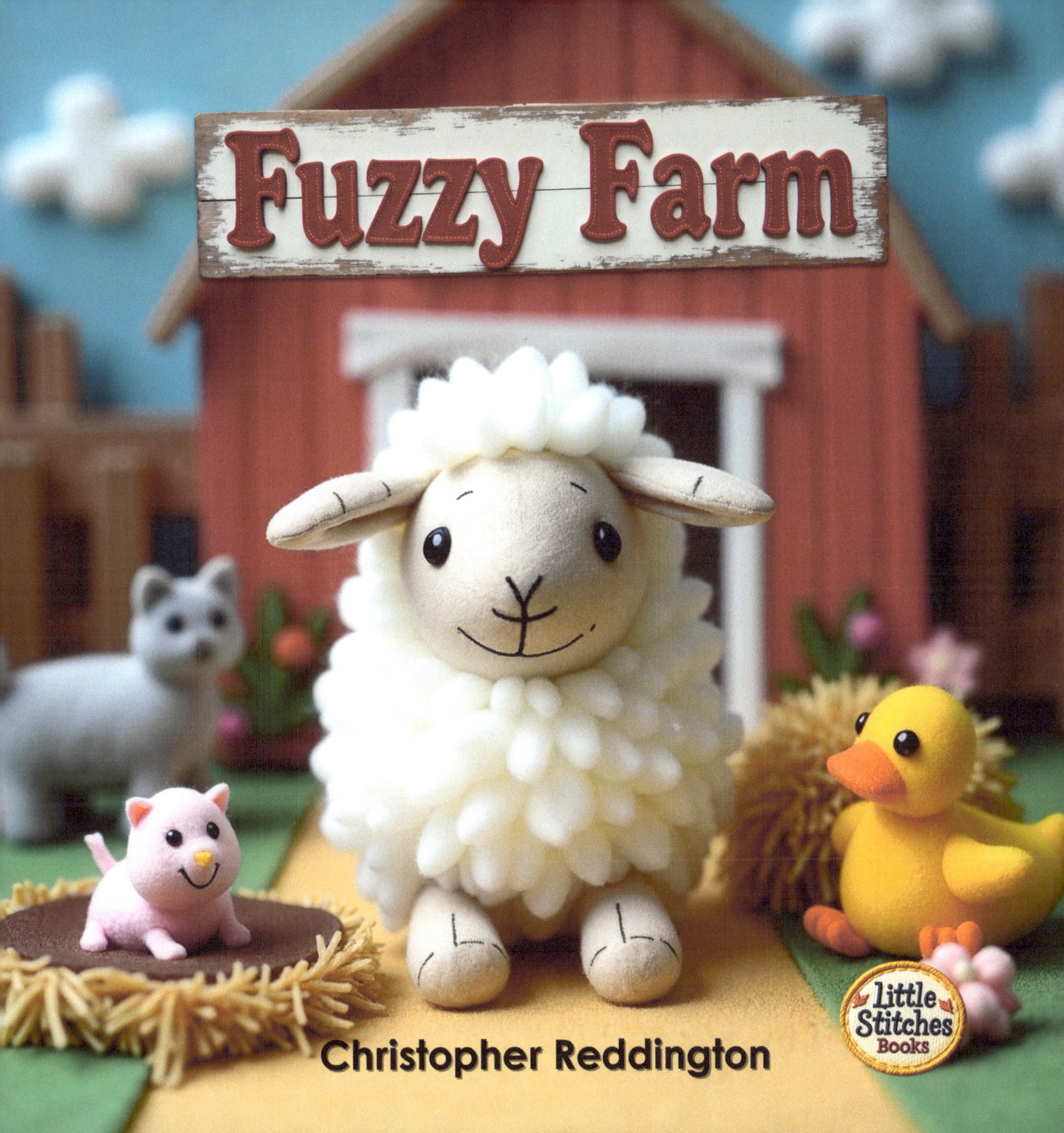

# Hi Friends!

Welcome, welcome, step on in,
Where fluffy wool and fun begin!

The farm is ready, the sky is blue,
All of my friends are excited for you!

So come on by, please don't wait,
Let's meet the farmyard, it will be great!

## Cow
# A '<u>Moo</u>' to you!

Out in the pasture, calm and sweet,
I munch and crunch my leafy treat.

The sun is warm, the grass is green,
And fluffy clouds drift through the scene.

So sit with me, relax a while,
And meet a cow with a '<u>Moo</u>' and a smile!

*Horse*
# Hello <u>Neigh</u>bour!

Step inside, don't be shy,
I'll greet you with a twinkling eye!

In my stable, safe and warm,
I rest and snack through rain or storm.

A crunchy apple, crisp and sweet,
The perfect little farmyard treat!

*Goose and Gosling*

# <u>Honk</u>, step, splash!

The sun dips low, the sky glows bright,
A golden end to day's delight.

Beside the stream, we waddle near,
My little one stays close and dear.

The water shimmers, soft and slow,
Let's take a stroll before we go!

*Cat and mouse*
# A <u>Purr</u>fect nap!

Curled up tight in golden hay,
I snooze and stretch the day away.

A ball of yarn, a cozy heap,
The barn is warm, it's time to sleep.

But hush, look close, and you might see,
A tiny friend who naps with me!

*Duck*

# <u>Q*uack*</u> along with me!

I glide gently, on my favorite pond
The water is calm, of that I'm fond.

Water lilies float, the breeze is sweet,
And frogs hop by with nimble feet - '<u>*ribbit*</u>!'

The dock is warm, the reeds stand tall,
Join me here, we'll 'Q<u>*uack*</u>' and call!

*Goat*

# <u>Baa</u>-lance and play!

Up on my rock, I stand so tall,
With my toy tin can, hear it call!

Crunchy snacks, I'm ready to share,
The veggie cart is full and fair.

I'll jump and play and bleat with glee,
Come on now, say '<u>*Baaaa*</u>' with me!

## Donkey
# Let's go, Hee-Haw!

I stand by my cart, the hay looks yummy,
It's stacked up so high, ready for my tummy.

The barn ahead, just down the way,
I'll pull the cart through bright sunray.

The road winds gently, soft and slow,
Walk with me now, we're ready to go!

### Rabbit
# Hop, Hop, Hop on by!

Down in my burrow, cozy and deep,
I munch on carrots before I sleep.

Soft earth around, bed made of fur ,
It's peaceful here, nobody stirs!

I'll twitch my nose, I'll wiggle my ears,
Hop on by friend, there's nothing to fear!

*Sheepdog*
# <u>Woof</u> and work!

I'm quick and nimble, watch me go,
Guiding the flock, to and fro.

With fluffy sheep and wagging tail,
I round them up, we never fail.

In the enclosure, we work as one,
The job is done, now time for fun!

*Turkey*

# Gobble on the go!

In the pumpkin patch, I waddle with pride,
The field is calm, the house is nearby.

The scarecrow watches, standing still,
While I puff my feathers, feeling a thrill.

Come speak with me, give a '*gobble*' or two,
I'll dance and twirl, just for you!

**Pig**

# <u>Oin</u>king in the mud!

In my muddy pool, I'm happy and bright,
As the sun sets low, with colors so right.

The windmill spins, the sky turns gold,
I splash around, feeling bold.

I roll and squish, so full of glee,
Take a deep breath then '<u>Oink</u>' with me!

*Llama*

# Llama time!

I stand by the fence, so fluffy and prim,
With a bucket of water filled up to the brim.

Two little birds perch, they chirp away,
With feathers so nice, they sing all day!

I'll stretch my neck, and give a smile,
Enjoying the sun and resting awhile!

### Hen
# <u>Cluck</u> and cuddle!

In my cozy coop, I sit so still,
On my eggs, keep them warm with skill.

A little hatchling, peeks out with glee,
New friends are coming, just wait and see!

I '<u>*Cluck*</u>' so softly, and enjoy the quiet,
Once my chicks are hatched, it will be quite a riot!

### Rooster
# Cock-a-doodle-doo!

I stand on the fence, so proud and tall,
The new sun rises, shining over all.

The barn looks cozy, the sky turns bright,
A new day begins, with morning light.

I crow loud and clear, no sleeping through,
Come hear my song, '*Cock-a-doodle-doo*!'

# Goodbye for now!

Thanks for coming, the tour is done,
I'm so glad we had some fun!

I've met you, friend, of that I'm happy,
But I must say goodbye, it's time for my nappy!

We laughed and played, had fun all day,
Don't worry, I'll see you again soon... okay?

LittleStitchesBooks.com

www.ingramcontent.com/pod-product-compliance
Lightning Source LLC
Chambersburg PA
CBHW041440010526
44118CB00002B/136